ZooBorns

THE NEXT GENERATION

Newer, Cuter, More Exotic Animals from the World's Zoos and Aquariums

Andrew Bleiman and Chris Eastland

SIMON & SCHUSTER

New York   London   Toronto   Sydney   New Delhi

Simon & Schuster
1230 Avenue of the Americas
New York, NY 10020

First Simon & Schuster hardcover edition November 2012

SIMON & SCHUSTER and colophon are registered trademarks
of Simon & Schuster, Inc.

For information about special discounts for bulk purchases,
please contact Simon & Schuster Special Sales at
1-866-506-1949 or business@simonandschuster.com.

The Simon & Schuster Speakers Bureau can bring authors
to your live event. For more information or to book an event,
contact the Simon & Schuster Speakers Bureau at
1-866-248-3049 or visit our website at www.simonspeakers.com.

Designed by Chris Eastland

Manufactured in China

10 9 8 7 6 5 4 3 2 1

Library of Congress Control Number 2012940189
ISBN 978-1-4516-6161-3
ISBN 978-1-4516-6162-0 (ebook)

For my wife, Lillian, and my brother, and fellow animal nerd, Ben.—A.B.

For Eloise and Lander.—C.E.

ZooBorns

THE NEXT GENERATION

Introduction

Like all the adorable youngsters featured in this book, Siku, the polar bear cub on the cover, is much more than just a cute, furry face. His name means "sea ice" in the Inuit language, and he is an ambassador for his species in the wild.

Across the Arctic, sea ice is melting earlier each spring and freezing later each fall. Polar bears depend on sea ice to reach the prey that sustains them. Of the twelve well-studied populations of polar bears, eight are currently declining. Research shows, however, that **it's not too late to take action** to save sea ice and polar bears by greatly reducing greenhouse gas emissions.

What can you do to help? Simply put, we must Build Green, Live Green, and Choose Green. The daily decisions that each of us make—from purchasing locally grown fruits and vegetables to conducting an energy audit and following the recommendations—add up to offer the best hope for the survival of polar bears and many other species, if we all commit to them.

Polar Bears International and the Association of Zoos and Aquariums (AZA) have teamed up on a Climate Initiative to raise awareness amongst zoo visitors about climate change and educate them on ways to reduce their impact. If you'd like to learn more about how you can help polar bears, visit or contact your local AZA accredited zoo or aquarium or visit the Polar Bears International website at www.PolarBearsInternational.org.

A portion of all proceeds from ZooBorns book sales goes directly to the AZA's Conservation Endowment Fund

Species: Polar Bear

Name: Siku

Home: Scandinavian Wildlife Park, Denmark

Born: 11.22.2011

Status: Vulnerable

3

Siku got off to a rough start when mother polar bear, Ilka, could not produce enough milk to feed her hungry young cub. Three days after his birth, keepers made the difficult decision to bottle-feed Siku. Since then, the playful cub has thrived under 24-hour human care, although he has proven to be most rambunctious at night, to the sleepy keepers' chagrin. Reintegration of Siku with the Zoo's other five polar bears will be a gradual process over the next two years.

Polar bears are the only bears classified as marine mammals because they spend so much of their life at sea, like their main prey, seals.

4

The cub's name, Siku, means "sea ice" in the Eskimo and Inuit languages. The name is symbolic, because polar bears are dependent on sea ice for survival. No sea ice means no seals, which means no polar bears. Scientists project we could lose two-thirds of the world's polar bears by midcentury and all of them by the end of the century.

Polar Bears International works to protect this iconic species through research, education, fundraising and advocacy.

POLAR BEARS
INTERNATIONAL

6

If you'd like to learn more about how you can support the critical efforts to save polar bears in the wild, visit www.polarbearsinternational.org.

Species: Lesser Mouse Deer
Home: Paignton Zoo, U.K.
Born: 6.19.2010
Status: Least Concern

Shortly before this tiny mouse deer was born, its mother lay critically ill on the operating table. After multiple surgeries to cure a long and complicated illness, she ultimately recovered and gave birth to a healthy fawn thanks to the hard work of Paignton Zoo veterinarians. Neither mouse nor deer, the lesser mouse deer is part of a unique family of small, primitive, hoofed mammals called chevrotains.

Species: Dingo

Home: Fort Wayne Children's Zoo, Indiana

Born: 1.30.2012

Status: Vulnerable

Pure dingoes are increasingly rare in the wild due to hybridization with domestic dogs. The Fort Wayne Children's Zoo was thrilled when they received Naya and Mattie, one of the estimated 75 pairs of pure dingoes worldwide. All three color phases of dingo are represented in this litter: the typical ginger color which blends with the red dirt of the Outback, the cream-colored coat, found on dingoes that inhabit the mountainous areas, and the black-and-tan coat color of dingoes that live in the forests.

Cheryl Piropato / Fort Wayne Children's Zoo

11

Species: Sambirano Lesser Bamboo Lemur
Name: Hamish
Home: Banham Zoo, U.K.
Born: August 2010
Status: Vulnerable

A Banham Zoo keeper stepped in to care for orphan lemur, Hamish, after the infant was rejected by his mother. After five months of care, including milk feedings day and night, Hamish was healthy and mature enough to get his own space right alongside his family and spends his days leaping from branch to branch and munching on bamboo shoots.

12

Banham Zoo

Species: Numbat

Home: Perth Zoo, Australia

Born: January 2010

Status: Endangered

The Perth Zoo breeds the endangered numbat for release back into the wild. This baby marks the first time this species has been successfully hand-raised from such a young age. Unlike most marsupials, the numbat is most active by day, spending its waking hours hunting for delicious termites (and only termites). While most termite eaters use powerful claws to dig up their prey's fortified mounds, the numbat relies on its powerful sense of smell to find shallow, accessible spots in the nest.

Species: Meerkat

Home: Point Defiance Zoo, Takoma, Washington

Born: March 2012

Status: Least Concern

In March of 2012, the Point Defiance Zoo welcomed a litter of four meerkat pups. Highly social, meerkats live in groups called mobs typically comprising about 20 individuals but sometimes reaching 50 or more. Both parents and relatives often chip in to help raise the young.

When the group goes foraging, at least one meerkat acts as a sentinel, keeping a lookout from a high perch for predators like hawks, eagles, and jackals.

Seth Bynam / Point Defiance Zoo & Aquarium

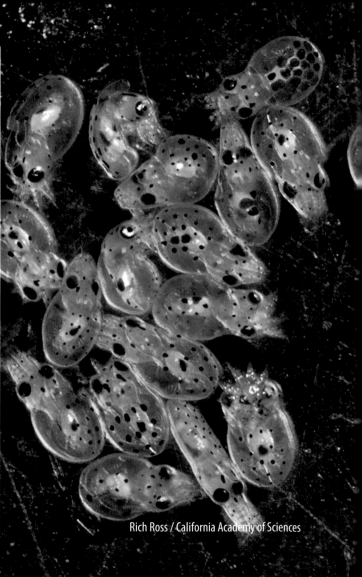

Species: Caribbean *Octopus vulgaris*
Home: California Academy of Sciences
Born: February 2011
Status: Least Concern

Shortly after putting their new Caribbean octopus on display, biologists at the California Academy of Sciences were surprised when she relocated under a rock and started laying eggs. This species is "small egged," and when the babies hatch they are no bigger than specks of dust at 1–2 mm in length. This photo was taken with the aid of a macro lens.

Rich Ross / California Academy of Sciences

Chris Humphries / Linton Zoo

Species: Brazilian Tapir

Home: Linton Zoo, U.K.

Born: 6.2.2010

Status: Vulnerable

This tapir calf marked the eleventh successful birth for proud and productive tapir parents Shannon and Tanya. In the wild, Brazilian tapirs are shy animals that spend much of their day partially submerged in marshes out of reach of jaguars. When threatened, the tapir can use its flexible snout like a snorkel and hide out underwater for hours at a time.

Mehgan Murghy / Smithsonian National Zoological Park

Species: Giant Anteater

Name: Pablo

Home: Smithsonian National Zoo, Washington, D.C.

Born: 12.7.2010

Status: Vulnerable

The largest species of anteater, giant anteaters have no teeth. Instead they use their sticky 2-foot-long tongues, which can zip in and out of their mouths over 150 times per minute, to gobble up insects, which are ground up between hard plates in their mouths and stomachs.

At over 7 feet long from nose to tail, giant anteaters are formidable animals and do not run from predators. Instead they stand on their hind legs and lash out with their claws or even "bear hug" their enemies.

Bottle-feeding takes on a whole new level of complexity when you have a face like little Pablo. Here's how Zoo staff describe it: *Nursing is a skill that in most mammals can be taken for granted, but think about what an anteater looks like and just how long that tongue is. Where does it go while the baby is nursing? Where do you put the hole in the nipple on the baby bottle so that the tongue doesn't block it? (Answer: you make lots of holes.) Ideally, the baby sticks his tongue all the way out and kind of over to the side. When the baby sucks the milk into its mouth, swallowing requires some movement of the tongue. What you end up with looks like fairly normal nursing except that there appears to be a small dark snake flailing around in the middle of it all.*

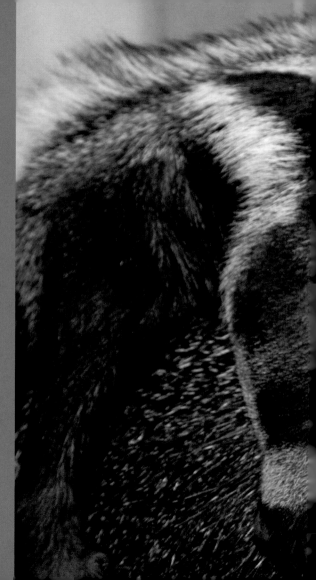

Species: Bonobo

Name: Lopori

Home: Twycross Zoo, United Kingdom

Born: 1.6.2012

Status: Endangered

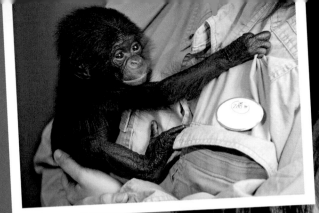

Little Lopori's natural mother, Maringa, was not an attentive parent, so Twycross Zoo keepers hand-raised her until she was strong enough to be paired with her foster mom, auntie Diatou.

Living in groups of 100 or more and sleeping in tree-top nests, bonobos are highly social and surprisingly laid-back apes, rarely exhibiting aggression toward one another. Along with the common chimpanzee, bonobos are humans' closest living relatives, sharing 99.6% of our DNA.

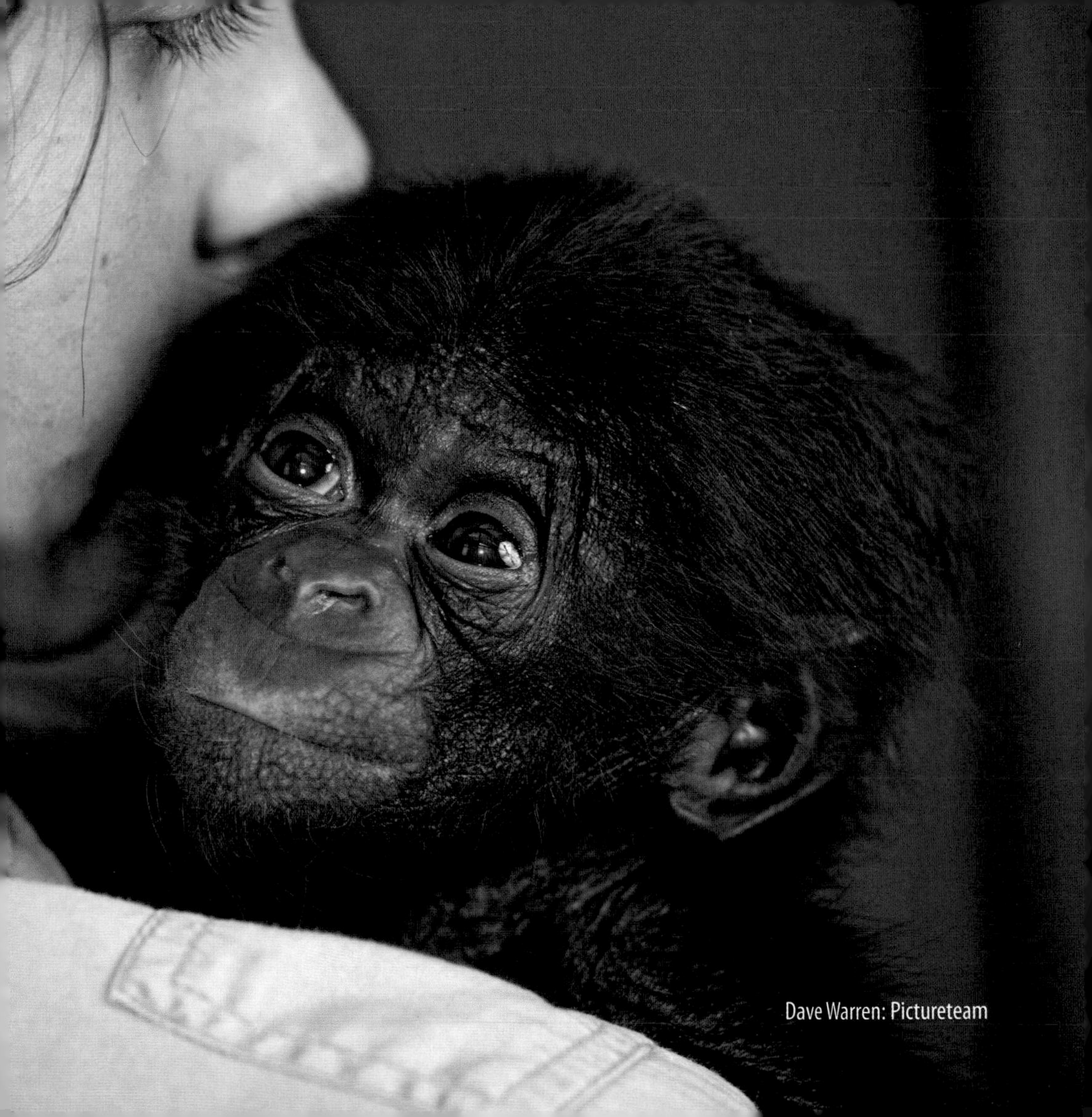
Dave Warren: Pictureteam

Species: American Manatee

Name: Valentine

Home: Singapore Zoo

Born: 2.13.2012

Status: Vulnerable

The birth of Valentine marks mother Eva's seventh calf born at the Singapore Zoo, no small feat for a species that typically gives birth to just one calf every two years after a 12-month gestation period.

While newborn manatees typically stick close to mom's side for the first 1–2 years, little Valentine began independently exploring his pool and investigating the other manatees just weeks after birth.

Species: Polynesian Tree Snail

Home: Marwell Wildlife Park, United Kingdom

Born: December 2011

Status: Extinct in the Wild

Native only to a handful of isolated islands in the Pacific Ocean, the Polynesian tree snail was wiped out in the wild when an aggressive, nonnative snail from Florida was misguidedly introduced to the islands in the 1970s. Marwell Wildlife Park breeds these delicate snails and releases them back into the wild with the aim of eventually re-populating the species.

Marwell Wildlife

Species: Eurasian Eagle Owl

Name: Caspian

Home: Cincinnati Zoo
& Botanical Garden, Ohio

Born: 3.30.2011

Status: Least Concern

While Caspian may be fluffy and awkward as a chick, as an adult he could have a wingspan six feet long, making him fully capable of hunting small deer. Eurasian eagle owls have one of the widest territories of any raptor, ranging from Korea and Japan all the way across continents to Northern Africa, France, and Spain.

Species: Pygmy Hippopotamus

Name: Prince Harry

Home: Cango Wildlife Ranch, South Africa

Born: 3.22.2012

Status: Endangered

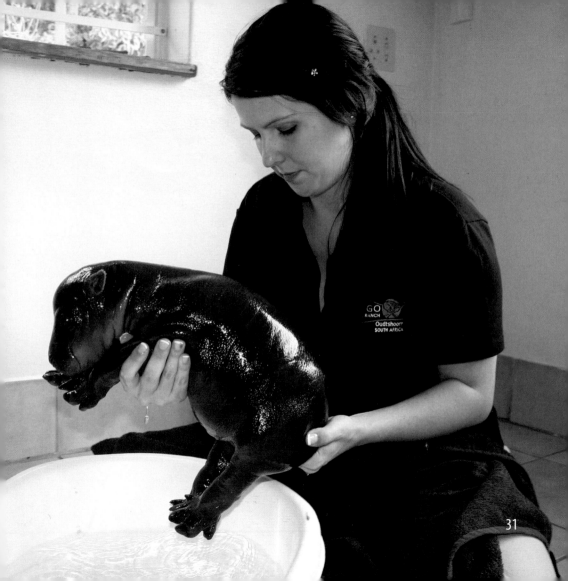

Staff at Cango Wildlife Ranch were eagerly anticipating the arrival of Prince Harry and took all the right steps to ensure a successful birth, including draining the pond so the calf wasn't born underwater. Despite their preparations, the labor was still a 12-hour ordeal that left keepers and hippo mom Hilda exhausted.

Unlike their confident full-sized cousins, pygmy hippos are shy forest dwellers that often live in burrows along riverbanks. Their reclusive and nocturnal nature combined with their small size make the pygmy hippo notoriously difficult to study in the wild. Most of what researchers know about this species comes from observing them at zoos.

Until recently, hippopotamuses were believed to be related to pigs and hogs, but recent genetic research confirms that whales and dolphins are their closest living relatives!

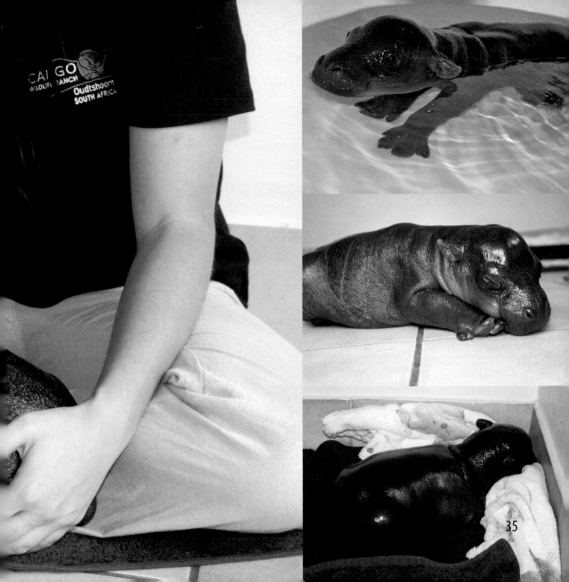

35

Species: Coquerel's Sifaka

Name: Nero

Home: The Maryland Zoo in Baltimore

Born: 11.12.2011

Status: Endangered

Weighing 95 grams at birth, about the same as a deck of cards, little Nero spent his first month clinging tight to mom's belly, then graduated to riding on her back. At two months, sifakas already have their trademark spring in their step, bouncing along the ground and hopping from branch to branch. As adults, they can leap twenty feet in a single bound!

Like many species of lemur, Coquerel's sifaka is endangered in its native Madagascar due to habitat destruction from logging and farming.

The Maryland Zoo in Baltimore

Species: Virginia Opossum

Name: Baby Opossum

Home: Virginia Living Museum, Virginia

Born: 2011

Status: Least Concern

Karl Rebenstorf / Virginia Living Museum

This orphaned baby opossum was rescued after her mother was killed by a passing car. She is being hand-raised, literally, by museum staff, who hope that this little marsupial will someday join the institution's animal education program, which introduces school-children to native species.

Species: Vicuña

Home: Chester Zoo, United Kingdom

Born: February 2010

Status: Least Concern

The national animal of Peru, vicuñas represent a tremendous conservation success story. In the 1960s, wild vicuña populations had fallen to just 6,000 individuals after hundreds of years of overhunting. Luckily, a coordinated conservation effort by the Peruvian government, World Wildlife Fund, Peace Corps, Nature Conservancy, and others established a refuge and Game Warden Academy to protect this species. Today the wild population has rebounded to over 350,000 vicuñas.

George Griffiths taken at Chester Zoo

Alaska SeaLife Center Staff

Species: Harbor Seal

Name: Gouda

Home: Alaska SeaLife Center

Born: 5.7.2011

Status: Least Concern

Found alone on the beach at just four days old, Gouda was transported to the Alaska SeaLife Center where she received much-needed fluids and electrolytes. After five months of exercise and training to catch her own fish under the direction of experienced wildlife rehabbers, Gouda was released back into the wild.

Species: Capybara

Home: San Diego Zoo, California

Born: 11.28.2011

Status: Least Concern

The world's largest rodent can reach 150 lbs and 4.5 feet long at maturity but starts life about the size of a guinea pig at just 3–4 lbs.

Capybara means "master of grasses" in the Guaraní language of South America and *hydrochaeris*, their Latin name, means "water hog." Both are apt titles for a species that loves nothing more than munching its way through a flooded field or lounging partially submerged in a jungle pond.

Highly social, capybaras live in large, talkative groups of up to 100 chirping, clicking, snorting, and barking individuals. These vocalizations help capybaras form social bonds, establish dominance, and reach group consensus.

Species: Somali Wild Ass

Name: Hakaba

Home: Zoo Basel, Switzerland

Born: 11.16.2010

Status: Critically Endangered

44

In these photos, a young foal named Hakaba explores her enclosure for the first time, cautiously sniffing then exuberantly running! The Somali Wild Ass is believed to be the ancestor of most domestic donkeys.

Among the rarest mammals, the Somali wild ass is critically endangered in the wild. Fortunately some 200 Somali wild asses live in zoos around the world, 35 of which were bred at Switzerland's Zoo Basel. Someday this population may be instrumental in repopulating the species in Ethiopia, Eritrea, and Somalia.

Species: Northern White-cheeked Gibbon

Name: Nakai

Home: Perth Zoo, Australia

Born: 4.17.2011

Status: Critically Endangered

When Nakai's mother had difficulty caring for him shortly after birth, Perth Zoo keepers stepped in and provided round-the-clock care, including baby milk formula feedings nine times throughout the day and night. Happily, Nakai was successfully reunited with his family group just a few months later. Keepers said it was as if Nakai and his mother, Viann, had never been apart.

49

While under the keeper's care, Nakai had a daily exercise regimen, including stretches and swinging by his arms to strengthen his upper body and encourage natural gibbon behavior.

In the wild, habitat destruction and poaching, particularly for the illegal pet trade, has had a devastating impact on white-cheeked gibbons, which now face a very high probability of extinction in the wild. Formerly distributed throughout China, Vietnam, and Laos, they are now completely extinct in China and virtually extinct in Vietnam, with just a few small populations remaining in Laos.

Perth Zoo is part of a regional breeding program for the critically endangered white-cheeked gibbon. Nakai was the 8th of her kind born at Perth Zoo.

Species: Tiger (Sumatran)

Names: Indah & Bugara

Home: Cameron Park Zoo, Waco, Texas

Born: 8.15.2011 and 8.16.2011

Status: Critically Endangered

Sheri Hemrick / Cameron Park Zoo

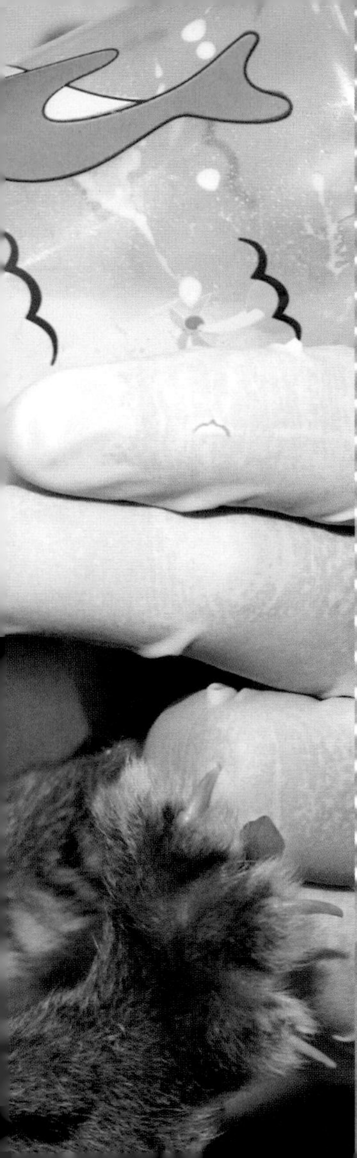

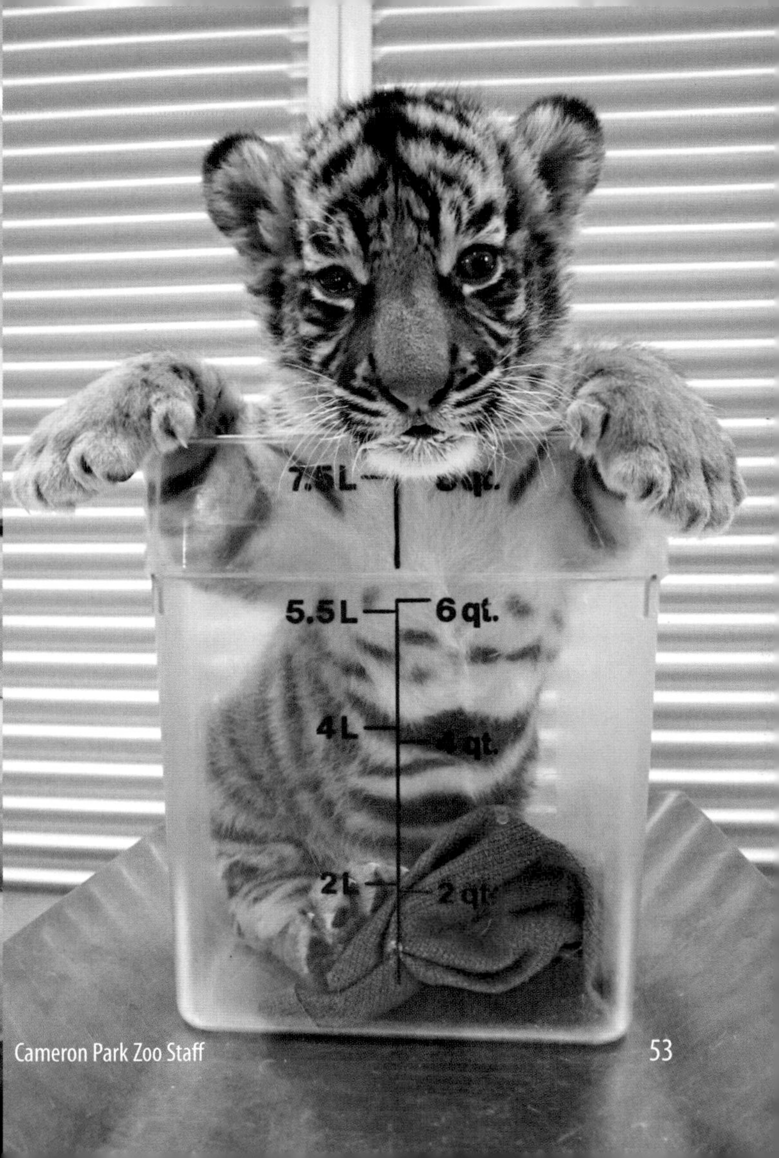

Cameron Park Zoo Staff

Cameron Park Zoo keepers have their hands full with Sumatran tiger cubs Indah (female) and Bugara (male).

This was the first litter for mother Maharani, and, unfortunately, she did not properly care for her cubs. Keepers stepped in to play surrogate tiger mom, bottle-feeding the cubs every few hours and ending their shifts covered in scratches. Tiger cubs love to play, but they play with sharp claws and teeth!

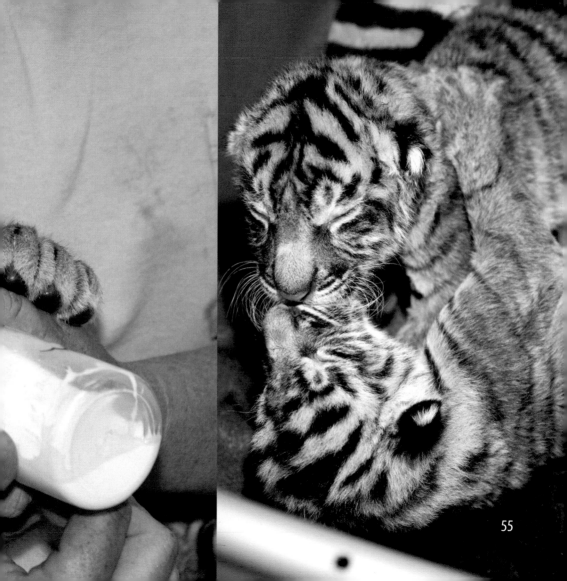

56

Sumatran tigers are the world's smallest and the only surviving member of a group of island tigers, which once included the Bali and Javan tigers. Despite the establishment of a large nature preserve on Sumatra, this population continues to decline due to poaching and deforestation for palm oil production.

Species: Maned Wolf

Names: Amazon, Pepe, and Miranda

Home: Norden's Ark, Sweden

Born: 1.19.2012

Status: Near Threatened

Tom Svensson / Norden's Ark

Although often described as a "fox on stilts," the maned wolf is not closely related to any other living fox, wolf, or dog. Unlike most other large canids, the maned wolf is solitary and also quite smelly, giving it another nickname, "skunk wolf."

Maned wolves are threatened in the wild by poachers and ranchers. With only a small number living at zoos, the birth of this litter is a notable accomplishment for Norden's Ark and the European Breeding Program.

Species: Pygmy Slow Loris

Names: Cai & Nam

Home: Moody Gardens, Texas

Born: 6.13.2012

Status: Vulnerable

Moody Gardens®

Twins Cai and Nam spent their first few weeks close to mother Luyen's side for nursing and comfort. As adults these pygmy slow lorises will live up to their name, weighing only a pound or less and moving cautiously from branch to branch as if in slow motion. Primitive primates, lorises rely on their humanlike hands and huge eyes to hunt tasty insects at night.

Pygmy slow lorises are vulnerable to extinction due to poaching for traditional medicine and the international pet trade.

Species: Common Wombat
Name: Mirrhi
Home: Taronga Zoo, Australia
Born: 2010
Status: Least Concern

This baby wombat, named Mirrhi, was rescued from the side of the highway after her mother was struck by a car. Requiring round-the-clock care, Mirrhi spent her days in Taronga Wildlife Hospital and went home with a wildlife nurse for overnights. Typically nocturnal, wombat joeys are most playful and adventurous at night, making them a tiresome handful for human surrogate moms to care for.

Lorinda Taylor / Taronga Zoo

Wombats like Mirrhi are built for digging, with big teeth and powerful paws. These specialized marsupials even have a backward facing pouch, so dirt doesn't get inside when they are burrowing. While this species is not endangered, wombats are slow breeders, only giving birth to one joey every two years.

Species: Fossa

Names: Ingrid & Gretchen

Home: Houston Zoo, Texas

Born: 6.25.2011

Status: Vulnerable

70

When Rianna (not pictured) was a young pup, her mother exhibited aggression toward her, and keepers separated the two after only a few days. So Houston Zoo staff breathed a sigh of relief when Rianna had her own litter and proved to be a caring but laid-back mom to her babies, Ingrid and Gretchen.

The fossa's appearance, agility, and stealth bear striking resemblance to that of felines, but in fact this species is more closely related to mongooses than cats. As Madagascar's apex predator, fossas have little to fear as they prowl amongst the treetops on the hunt for their next lemur dinner.

71

Species: Bongo (Eastern)

Name: Brody

Home: Houston Zoo, Texas

Born: 12.6.2011

Status: Critically Endangered

Brody, the baby bongo, was a big boy, weighing in at 40 lbs at birth, but his healthy appetite helped him reach a whopping 92 lbs only five weeks later! To distinguish the fast-growing Brody from other bongos in the Houston Zoo herd, keepers count the number of stripes on his side.

Eastern bongo populations have declined sharply due to a triple threat from hunting, de-forestation and disease passed along from domestic livestock. Today only 75–140 Eastern bongos are estimated to live in the wild, meaning this subspecies is critically endangered. Luckily over 400 Eastern bongos live in North American zoos. Breeding programs, like those at the Houston Zoo, may be the best hope for someday rebuilding populations in the wild.

Native to the lowlands and mountain forests of Kenya and western Africa, bongos are the only forest antelope to form herds. However, when it comes to humans, this species is shy and elusive, making them difficult to track down in the wild.

Species: Giant Otter

Home: Zoo Miami, Florida

Born: 1.31.2011

Status: Endangered

Ron Magill / Zoo Miami

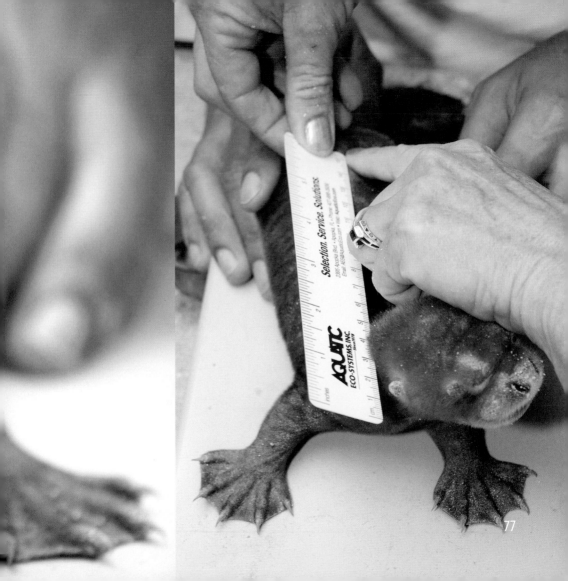

These two giant otter pups, one male and one female, represent the second time in history that this species has been successfully bred at a North American zoo. This landmark event was the culmination of years of collaboration between Zoo Miami, the Philadelphia Zoo, the Cali Zoo in Colombia, and the Brazilian Institute of the Environment.

Giant otters can be sensitive to external activity, so Zoo Miami staff let the parents and pups bond in seclusion for a month before briefly removing the babies for their first veterinary exam. The pups weighed in at 2–3 lbs; a far cry from their mature weight of nearly 75 lbs and length of 6 feet or more!

Commonly called "river wolves" in their native South America, giant otters feed mainly on fish but have been known to eat snakes and even caimans, a smaller cousin of the alligator.

Giant otters are highly social and surprisingly noisy, living in family groups of 10–20 chatty individuals. Humming, whining, barking, and growling are all common in giant otter communication. These vocalizations are used to warn the group of danger, alert them to food, or comfort one another, among other purposes.

Species: Leopard Tortoise

Names: Chablis, Sancerre, Tokaji, Champagne, Prosecco, Sherry, & Veltlín a Pinot

Home: Prague Zoo, Czech Republic

Born: 1.1.2012

Status: Least Concern

83

When Prague Zoo herpetologists discovered that leopard tortoise eggs develop best in cool temperatures, they transformed a wine refrigerator into the perfect climate-controlled incubator. Fittingly the first tortoise hatchlings out of the fridge received vinology-inspired names: Chablis, Sancerre, Tokaji, Champagne, Prosecco, Sherry, and Veltlín a Pinot.

Captive breeding of this species, one of the world's largest tortoises, has reduced poaching of wild leopard tortoises for the pet trade.

85

Species: Honey Badger

Name: B.G. (aka Badger Guy)

Home: Johannesburg Zoo, South Africa

Born: 11.18.2010

Status: Least Concern

Feisty, stubborn, smelly, and adventurous, at 14 weeks old this honey badger cub exhibited all the trademark charms of his species.

Despite the "sweet" name, honey badgers are notoriously fearless and, when necessary, ferocious. They get their name for following the call of the honey guide bird to beehives. This partnership works well as the badger opens the beehive, brushing off the swarm of angry bees, and shares some of the spoils with the bird.

Lorna Fuller / Johannesburg Zoo

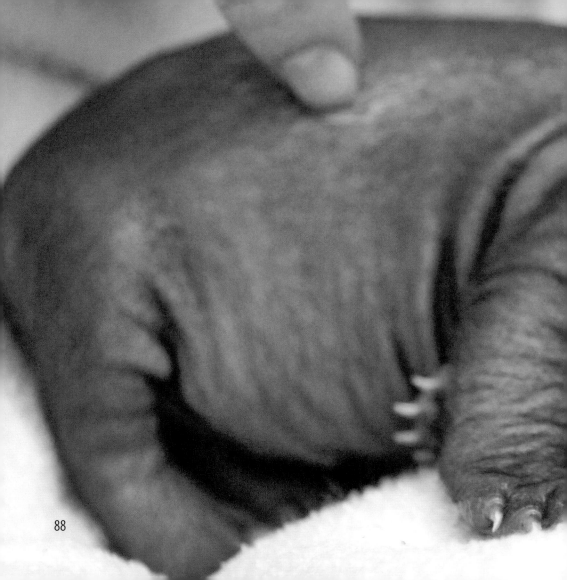

Badger Guy was an unexpected discovery in the den after his parents were moved to a different exhibit. Zoo staff shared this description: *He was raised on Royal Canine puppy formula and drank quite easily once the correct feeding nipple was found but proved to be very stubborn, only drinking when he needed to drink and not when you wanted him to do so. Now he is exhibiting the behavior of adult honey badgers, stalking guinea fowl in the Zoo, crawling with his tail upright and his belly low to the ground. He is extremely smelly and scent-marks everything and everyone.*

Species: Hoffmann's Two-toed Sloth

Name: Ruth

Home: Rosamond Gifford Zoo, New York

Born: August 2010

Status: Least Concern

Born underweight, Ruth bounced back thanks to keepers supplementing her nursing with nutritional formula. Now Ruth is happy, healthy, and as active as a two-toed sloth ought to be, which is to say, pretty laid back.

The sloth's shaggy coat and mellow lifestyle provide an ideal habitat for algae, giving the sloth's fur a greenish tinge and providing additional camouflage within the jungle canopy.

Amelia Beamish / Rosamond Gifford

92

Species: Giraffe (Rothschild)

Home: Dublin Zoo, Ireland

Born: 5.16.2011

Status: Endangered

Giraffes have a fifteen-month gestation period, and mothers give birth while standing up. This means giraffe babies fall 6 feet to the ground when they're born!

Patrick Bolger / Dublin Zoo

94

Standing 6 feet tall at birth, this newborn was a normal height for a healthy baby giraffe. He joins mother Hailey, father Robin and sister Kuliko along with five other giraffes in the Dublin Zoo's herd.

With only a few hundred members remaining in the wild, the Rothschild giraffe subspecies is among the most endangered of any giraffe. As the tallest land animals, adult giraffes have few predators, but they cannot protect themselves against ongoing habitat destruction by humans.

Species: Cheetah

Name: Kasi

Home: Busch Gardens, Tampa Bay, Florida

Born: 1.17.2011

Status: Vulnerable

Kasi was born at the Jacksonville Zoo, but his mother was unable able to care for him. The decision was made to move Kasi to Busch Gardens where they could provide dedicated 24-hour support.

97

Cheetah cubs are typically born in pairs, so keepers decided to introduce Kasi to a playpal, a Labrador retriever puppy named Mtani. The two playful youngsters are naturally curious and enjoy racing, romping, and roughhousing around the exhibit. Pairing puppies and single cheetah cubs together is not uncommon at zoos and these two will stay companions for life.

Species: Klipspringer

Home: Mesker Park Zoo & Botanic Garden, Indiana

Born: 1.6.2012

Status: Least Concern

This wobbly male calf will grow into a sure-footed adult who bounds confidently from rock to rock. Klipspringers are strictly monogamous, a rare trait amongst antelope species, and stay within feet of their mate at all times, taking turns eating and keeping watch for predators.

Jessica McCauley / Mesker Park Zoo & Botanic Garden

Species: Arctic Fox
Names: Kenai and Miki
Home: Aquarium of the Pacific, California
Born: May 2011
Status: Least Concern

During the winter, adult Arctic foxes sport bright white coats, perfect camouflage for their snow covered surroundings. In warmer months, their coats change to brown or blue-gray to match the mottled landscape. Weathering brutally frigid temperatures of -59° F or less means planning ahead, so Arctic foxes bury extra food in the snow and return to these natural freezers for dinner during lean times.

At just six weeks old, brothers Kenai and Miki exhibit the rambunctious playfulness typical of Arctic fox pups, also known as kits.

Species: Aye-aye

Name: Elphaba

Home: Duke Lemur Center, North Carolina

Born: 11.28.2011

Status: Near Threatened

106

Elphaba was the 28th aye-aye born at the Duke Lemur Center, and the healthy baby girl is purportedly "growing like a weed!" The aye-aye is the world's largest nocturnal primate and spends its nights hunting for juicy grubs living inside trees. Like all lemurs, the gentle aye-aye lives in Madagascar. Because of their strange appearance, aye-ayes are sometimes hunted by superstitious villagers who consider them bad omens.

David Haring / Duke Lemur Center

Species: Koala

Name: Pound

Home: Dreamworld, Australia

Born: 11.3.2010

Status: Least Concern

Dreamworld / Koala Country Photographics

In 2011, a banner year for koalas at Dreamworld in Australia, eleven joeys emerged from their mothers' pouches, including this little male, named Pound.

Like many marsupials, the koala has a short gestation period: only 34 days. Immediately after birth, the tiny, pink, hairless koala joey must find its way into mom's pouch, where it will spend the next six months nursing before venturing out.

Species: African Pygmy Hedgehog

Names: Mickey and Minnie

Home: Belfast Zoological Gardens, United Kingdom

Born: 8.30.2011

Status: Least Concern

Friendly and curious, Mickey (pictured on the right and with mom above) and Minnie now serve as popular outreach animals for the Belfast Zoo's Education Department, introducing over 40,000 children a year to the world of hedgehogs. When threatened, hedgehogs curl up into a ball and stick out their quills like a tennis ball combined with a cactus.

110

111

Species: South American Coati

Home: Melbourne Zoo, Australia

Born: 11.25.2011

Status: Least Concern

Melbourne only recently welcomed coatis to the Zoo, but the group settled in so well that they produced three litters back-to-back. This most recent litter of five baby coatis, called kittens, includes four females and one male.

Meagan Thomas, Melbourne Zoo

Coati females and young are highly social and live in groups of 10–20 individuals. Adult females look out for one another's kittens, assisting with grooming, feeding, and protecting them from predators when mom goes foraging.

Much like their raccoon cousins, coatis are omnivorous and will eat anything from insects, lizards, and rodents to nuts and fruits like the prickly pear, their favorite treat! In many areas of South America, coatis have become accustomed to handouts from tourists and will boldly climb visitors like a jungle gym to get at a snack.

Species: Geoffroy's Spider Monkey

Name: Estela

Home: Melbourne Zoo, Australia

Born: 1.17.2011

Status: Endangered

Trent Browning / Melbourne Zoo

Abandoned by her mother, little Estela was hand-raised by keepers at the Melbourne Zoo. Lacking the natural antibodies that would come from her mother's milk, Estela struggled with illness for the first few months of her life. Luckily, she pulled through and bonded with grandmother, Sonja, thanks to regular playtimes facilitated by the keepers.

Geoffroy's spider monkeys' prehensile tails help these large, agile monkeys swing confidently from tree to tree. A hairless pad at the end of the monkey's tail functions like a fifth hand, snatching up fruits and delivering them right to the hungry monkey's mouth.

Geoffroy's spider monkeys have been observed chewing up leaves from lime trees and rubbing the mixture on their fur: a natural insect repellent!

Species: Epaulette Shark

Home: New England Aquarium

Born: 1.24.2012

Status: Least Concern

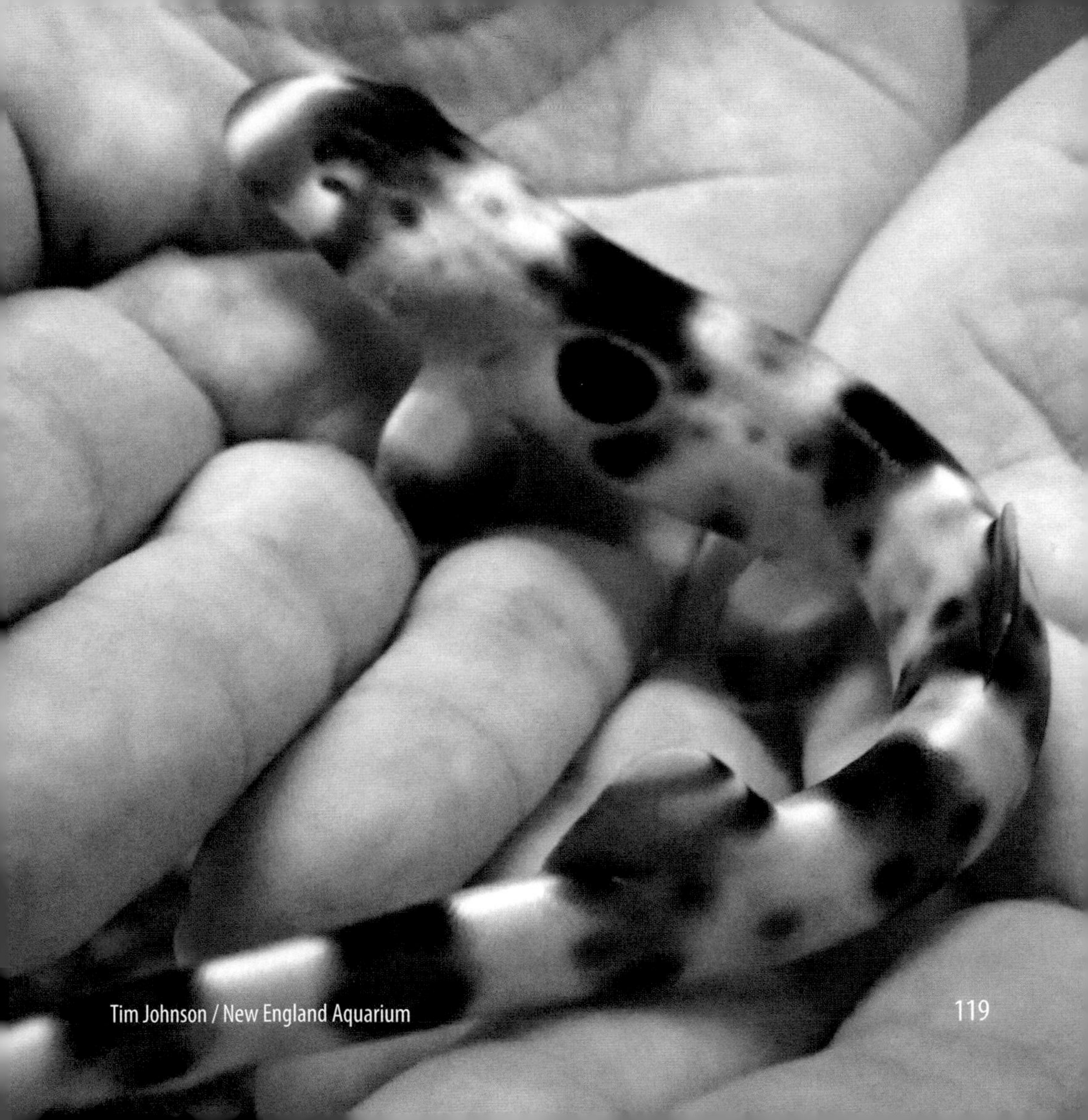

Tim Johnson / New England Aquarium

Aquarists at New England Aquarium were thrilled when this little lady hatched 151 days after her mother deposited her egg case (shown here).

Rather than swim, these sharks navigate their complex coral reef environments by "walking" between rocks and coral with their fins. They have also evolved to survive prolonged periods trapped in oxygen-poor tidepools, shutting off nonvital brain functions until the tide comes back in.

Newborn epaulette sharks have distinct stripes that let them blend into their surroundings. The stripes fade as the shark gets older and their sandy-colored body blends in with their sandy habitat, allowing their large dark spots to be easily seen. If a predator swims by, the shark's spots resemble the eyes of a larger animal, hopefully making the hunter think twice.

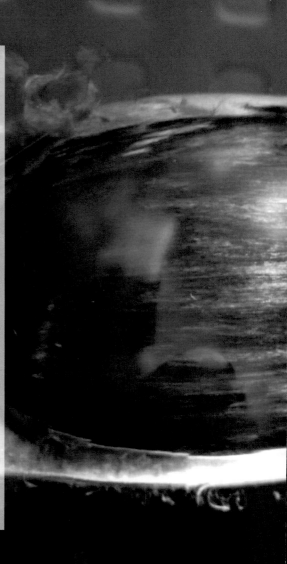

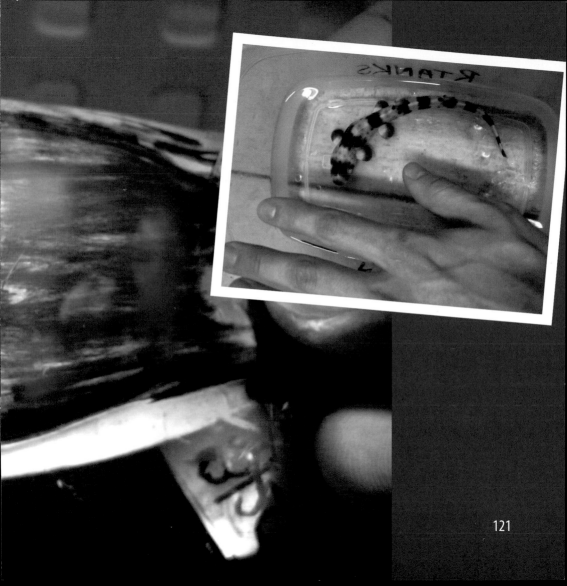

Species: Emu

Home: Busch Gardens, Tampa Bay, Florida

Born: 2.5.2012

Status: Least Concern

122

Busch Gardens' keepers knew when this emu chick was ready to hatch by pressing their ears to the shell and listening for the baby emu tapping on the inside. Standing just five inches tall at birth but reaching over 6.5 feet in adulthood, emus are the second-tallest bird after the ostrich. Emus' legs and claws are powerful enough to tear through metal fencing.

Jeroen Jacobs, taken at CRBGPB

Species: Giant Panda
Home: Chengdu Panda Base, China
Born: September 2010
Status: Endangered

124

Giant pandas are born quite helpless, with their eyes closed and no fur or teeth. They live with their mothers until they are almost two years old. Though pandas are beloved around the world, this species faces huge conservation challenges. The Chengdu Panda Base supports wildlife conservation efforts throughout China and works to maintain a viable, self-sustaining population of pandas as a hedge against extinction in the wild.

Jangala the dhole pup had to be hand-raised by keepers at Taronga Zoo but was eventually reintroduced to the adult group of dholes. Soon Jangala became so comfortable in the pack that he took the dominant male position from his own father!

Bobby-Jo Clow / Taronga Zoo

Species: Dhole
Name: Jangala
Home: Taronga Zoo, Australia
Born: 7.20.2007
Status: Endangered

More closely related to jackals than wolves, dholes once roamed across much of Asia but today they are confined to isolated pockets within India, Vietnam, Thailand and Myanmar. Unlike most wild canines, dholes allow their pups to eat first at mealtime.

Species: Przewalski's Horse

Name: Primula

Home: Prague Zoo, Czech Republic

Born: 8.2.2011

Status: Endangered

Most "wild horses" are descendants of domestic horses that escaped and grew feral over generations. However, Przewalski's horse is a truly wild subspecies that has never been domesticated.

© Tomáš Adamec / Prague Zoo

127

Native to the Mongolian steppes, these beautiful animals went extinct in the wild in the 1960s. Fortunately 45 Przewalski's horses were still living in zoos, descendants of wild animals that had been captured around 1900. Working with this tiny population, a multinational team began breeding and reintroduction efforts, which to date have restored the wild population from zero to 300 individuals.

This most recent foal was the 216th for the Prague Zoo, which continues its legacy of Przewalski's horse conservation and its record for the longest continuous breeding history worldwide.

Species: Squirrel Glider
Name: Corymbia
Home: Taronga Zoo, Australia
Born: 2011
Status: Least Concern

130

This orphaned squirrel glider joey was brought to the Taronga Zoo after being found on the side of the road. After round-the-clock care by a staff wildlife nurse, the joey made a full recovery and was moved to the Zoo's Nocturnal House.

The most striking feature of these small Australian marsupials is their patagium—a membrane that stretches from their hands to their feet, allowing them to glide over 100 yards or more, the length of a football field!

132

Species: Matschie's Tree Kangaroo

Name: Yawan

Home: Woodland Park Zoo, Seattle, Washington

Born: 12.6.2010

Status: Endangered

Like all Matschie's tree kangaroos, Yawan was born the size of a lima bean and spent months inside mom's pouch before taking a peek outside. In fact, zookeepers had to wait six months before catching a glimpse of little Yawan's head! Woodland Park Zoo is home to the Tree Kangaroo Conservation Program (TKCP), which works with local populations in Papua New Guinea's Huon Peninsula to protect this endangered species. Recently the TKCP had a breakthrough, establishing the nation's first-ever conservation area, comprising 180,000 acres of tree kangaroo habitat.

135

Species: Geoffroy's Marmoset

Home: Little Rock Zoo, Arkansas

Born: 11.21.2011

Status: Least Concern

Born on a stormy night to parents Becky and Santana, these healthy twins spend their days and nights riding on the backs of mom and dad (pictured). Older brother Carlos has also offered to carry the babies, but so far protective mom Becky has not allowed it. Native to Brazil, these small monkeys breed so prolifically in captivity that zoos often take steps to prevent it.

137

Species: Galápagos Giant Tortoise

Name: NJ

Home: Taronga Western Plains Zoo, Australia

Born: 3.19.2011

Status: Vulnerable

Mandy Quayle / Taronga Zoo

Little "NJ," the Galápagos Giant Tortoise hatchling, represents 10 years of breeding efforts by the Taronga Western Plains Zoo. He is the first of his species ever to be born in Asia or Australia.

The Galápagos Giant Tortoise is the largest tortoise species, weighing in at over 800 lbs. Just shy of 95 grams at birth, NJ was less than 0.033% of his mature size. One of the longest-living vertebrates on the planet, the oldest Galápagos Giant Tortoise on record lived to the ripe old age of 170, and that's only as far back as people kept track!

Species: Aardvark

Name: Zawadi

Home: Busch Gardens, Tampa Bay, Florida

Born: 4.10.2011

Status: Least Concern

This baby aardvark, named Zawadi, was hand-raised after Busch Gardens' keepers became concerned that his mother might accidentally step on him or even bury the cub in one of her daily digging sessions.

Neither the cleverest nor most coordinated of mammals, the aardvark is often called a living fossil as most of its close evolutionary cousins went extinct over 2.5 million years ago.

Aardvarks use their powerful claws like shovels to tear open termite mounds and dig up ant colonies. The aardvark then uses its 12-inch-long sticky tongue to slurp up as many as 50,000 insects in a single night. Extra thick skin protects the aardvark against angry bites and stings, and it can tightly close its nostrils to keep out dirt and insects. Given these unique adaptations, it's no wonder many Africans call them "antbears."

142

INDEX BY ANIMAL

INDEX BY ZOO

Thanks to the institutions and inviduals that made *ZooBorns* possible:

Aalborg Zoo
Adelaide Zoo
Akron Zoo
Al Ain Wildlife Park & Resort
Alaska SeaLife Center
Alma Park Zoo
Antwerp Zoo
Apenheul Primate Park
Aquarium of the Bay
Aquarium of the Pacific
Artis Zoo
Assiniboine Park Zoo
Auckland Zoo
Audubon Zoo
Australia Zoo
Aviarios Sloth Sanctuary
Banham Zoo
Belfast Zoo
Belgrade Zoo
Berlin Zoo
Besancon Zoo
Binder Park Zoo
Binghamton Zoo
Birch Aquarium
Blackpool Zoo
Bramble Park Zoo
Brevard Zoo
Bristol Zoo Gardens
British Wildlife Centre
Brookfield Zoo

Buffalo Zoo
Burgers Zoo
Busch Gardens
Calgary Zoo
California Academy of Sciences
Cango Wildlife Ranch
Cameron Park Zoo
Cape May County Zoo
Capron Park Zoo
Central Florida Zoo
Chattanooga Zoo
Chengdu Panda Base
Chessington Zoo
Chester Zoo
Chiang Mai Zoo
Chilean National Zoo
Cincinnati Zoo
Cleveland Metroparks Zoo
Colchester Zoo
Columbus Zoo & Aquarium
Como Zoo
Connecticut's Beardsley Zoo
Darmstadt Zoo
Denver Zoo
Detroit Zoo
Dierenrijk Europa Zoo
Diergaarde Blijdorp
Disney's Animal Kingdom
Dortmund Zoo
Dreamworld Australia

Dresden Zoo
Drusillas Park
Dublin Zoo
Dudley Zoo
Duke Lemur Center
Durrell Wildlife Conservation Trust
Dusit Zoo
Edinburgh Zoo
Edmonton Valley Zoo
Everland Zoo
Florida Aquarium
Fort Wayne Children's Zoo
Frankfurt Zoo
Georgia Aquarium
Great Plains Zoo
Hagenbeck Zoo
Hamilton Zoo
Hannover Zoo
Happy Hollow Zoo
Healesville Sanctuary
Hogle Zoo
Honolulu Zoo
Houston Zoo
Howlett's Wild Animal Park
Indianapolis Zoo
Jacksonville Zoo
Jardin des Plantes
Jerusalem Biblical Zoo
Johannesburg Zoo
Jurong Bird Park

Kangaroo Conservation Center
Kansas City Zoo
Knoxville Zoo
Kolmarden Zoo
Lakes Aquarium
Lee Richardson Zoo
Lincoln Children's Zoo
Lincoln Park Zoo
Linton Zoo
Lion Country Safari
Little Rock Zoo
Living Coasts Zoo
Longleat Safari Park
Loro Parque
Los Angeles Zoo
Louisville Zoo
Lowry Park Zoo
MacDuff Aquarium
Marwell Park Zoo
Maryland Zoo
Mata Ciliar Association
Melbourne Zoo
Memphis Zoo
Mesker Park Zoo
Mexicali Zoo
Milwaukee County Zoo
Minnesota Zoo
Mogo Zoo
Monkholm Zoo
Monterey Bay Aquarium
Moody Gardens
Mulhouse Zoo

Munster Zoo
Mystic Aquarium
M'Bopicuá Breeding Station
Naples Zoo
Nashville Zoo
National Aquarium in Baltimore
New England Aquarium
Newport Zoo
Newquay Zoo
Niabi Zoo
Norden's Ark
North Carolina Aquarium at Pine Knoll
Shores
North Carolina Zoo
Northeastern Wisconsin Zoo
Oakland Zoo
Odense Zoo
Oklahoma City Zoo
Omahas Henry Doorly Zoo
Opel Zoo
Oregon Zoo
Osaka Aquarium Kaiyukan
Ouwehands Zoo
Paignton Zoo
Palm Beach Zoo
Park of Legends
Perth Zoo
Philadelphia Zoo
Phoenix Zoo
Pittsburgh Zoo
Planckendael Zoo
Point Defiance Zoo

Potter Park Zoo
Prague Zoo
Puerto Vallarta Zoo
Red River Zoo
Rio Grande Zoo
Riverbanks Zoo
Rome's Biopark Zoo
Rosamond Gifford Zoo
Rotterdam Zoo
Sacramento Zoo
Safari West
Saint Louis Zoo
Salisbury Zoo
San Diego Zoo
San Francisco Zoo
Santa Barbara Zoo
Scandinavian Wildlife Park
Schoenbrunn Zoo
Schwerin Zoo
SeaWorld Orlando
SeaWorld San Diego
Secret World Wildlife Rescue Center
Shedd Aquarium
Singapore Zoo
Smithsonian National Zoo
Southwick's Zoo
St. Augustine Alligator Farm Zoological Park
Stockholm Zoo
Sunshine International Aquarium
Taipei Zoo
Tallinn Zoo

Tama Zoo
Taronga Zoo
Tel Aviv Zoological Center
Tennessee Aquarium
The Fund for Animals Wildlife Center
Toledo Zoo
Toronto Zoo
Trotter's World
Tulsa Zoo
Twycross Zoo
Ueno Zoo

Virginia Living Museum
Virginia Zoo
WCS's Bronx Zoo
WCS's New York Aquarium
WCS's Prospect Park Zoo
WCS's Queens Zoo
Wellington Zoo
Wildlife Heritage Foundation
Wildlife World Zoo
Wilhelma Zoo
Wingham Wildlife Park

Woodland Park Zoo
Wuppertal Zoo
Zoo Atlanta
Zoo Basel
Zoo Duisberg
Zoo Miami
Zoo New England
ZooAmerica
ZSL London Zoo
ZSL Whipsnade Zoo

ABOUT THE AUTHORS

Andrew Bleiman spends his days working in new media strategy and nights dreaming of ways to spend more time at zoos and aquariums. He graduated from the University of Pennsylvania with a degree in English literature and a yet to be recognized minor in baby animal-ology. Andrew lives in Chicago, Illinois, with his wife, Lillian, and their dogs, Izzy and Mathman.

Chris Eastland is a classically trained portrait artist and a freelance web and graphic designer. While Chris loves all the ZooBorns, he's particularly partial to primates and cats. He lives in Brooklyn with his cat, Georgie.

Andrew and Chris share a passion for connecting people and animals, and with *ZooBorns* they hope to raise awareness of the vital role zoos and aquariums play in conservation. To learn more about the animals in this book—and to meet even more zoo babies—visit their website, ZooBorns.com.

Don't miss all the other ZooBorns books, available wherever books are sold or at:

www.simonandschuster.com

And visit ZooBorns.com for the latest newborn arrivals!

www.zooborns.com